First
Resort

Straightforward, ready-to-use

worksheets and activities for

beginner students of English

Rosemary Picking

Margaret Prudden

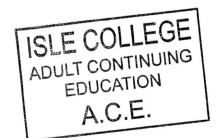

fully photocopiable

P & P Publications

Copyright

Permission to photocopy

Acknowledgements

Ethnic Minorities Language Service, Newcastle-upon-Tyne for their Dominoes Game idea
Sean Doogan for his artwork

Printed by

Photofix, Rainham, Essex

ISBN   1 898614 39 3

Introduction

As tutors, we have spent many hours making sets of alphabet letters, clocks and picture cards for our students. We have therefore produced these fully photocopiable worksheets which are ready for immediate use.

For each topic, there is an information sheet for the students to keep, followed by practice sheets in a variety of formats, including gap-filling, sentence completion and matching.
Some sheets are designed to be cut up into word cards and picture cards, for example 'clothes' and 'food'.
Other sheets provide a set of word cards to be matched with a large picture, for example 'body', 'face', 'family', 'house and garden' and 'rooms'

The coloured sheets will photocopy in black and white, if necessary. However, for 'colours' we have provided additional blank sheets ready for the tutor to colour in, if colour photocopying is not available.

We hope this resource will save you time and effort !

Contents

THE ALPHABET

BIG LETTERS

A   B   C   D   E   F   G

_   _   _   _   _   _   _

H   I   J   K   L   M   N

_   _   _   _   _   _   _

O   P   Q   R   S   T

_   _   _   _   _   _

U   V   W   X   Y   Z

_   _   _   _   _   _

the alphabet

small letters

a   b   c   d   e   f   g

—   —   —   —   —   —   —

h   i   j   k   l   m   n

—   —   —   —   —   —   —

o   p   q   r   s   t

—   —   —   —   —   —

u   v   w   x   y   z

—   —   —   —   —   —

A a A a _____

B b B b _____

C c C c _____

D d D d _____

E e E e _____

F f F f _____

G g G g _____

H h H h _____

I i I i _____

J j J j _____

K k K k _____

L l L l _____

M m M m _____

N n N n   _____

O o O o   _____

P p P p   _____

Q q Q q _____

R r R r   _____

S s S s   _____

T t T t   _____

U u U u _____

V v V v   _____

W w W w _____

X x X x   _____

Y y Y y   _____

Z z Z z _____

A B C D E F G H I J K L M N O P Q R S T U V W X Y Z

a b c d e f g h i j k l m n o p q r s t u v w x y z

A B C D E F G H I J K L M N O P Q R S T U V W X Y Z

a b c d e f g h i j k l m n o p q r s t u v w x y z

ALPHABETICAL ORDER   A - Z

A   B _ D   E   F   G _ I   J _ L   M   N _ P   Q _ S   T   U _ W   X _ Z

A _ C   D   E _ G   H _ J   K _ M _ O   P _ R   S _ U   V _ X   Y _

A _ C _ _ G   H _ _ _ L _ N _ _ _ R   S _ U   V _ X _ Z

_ B _ D _ F _ H _ J _ L _ N _ P _ R _ T _ V _ X _ Z

A _ _ _ F _ _ _ _ N _ _ _ S _ _ _ _ _ _

6

alphabetical order a - z

a _ c _ e _ _ h _ j k _ m _ o _ q r _ t _ v w _ y z

a b _ _ e f _ h _ i _ _ l m n _ p q _ _ t u _ w _ _ _

a _ c _ e _ g _ i _ k _ m _ o _ q _ s _ u _ w _ y _

_ b _ d _ f _ h _ j _ l _ n _ p _ r _ t _ v _ x _ z

a _ _ _ _ _ h _ _ _ m _ _ _ t _ _ _ _ _ _

A	B	C	D
E	F	G	H
I	J	K	L
M	N	O	P
Q	R	S	T
U	V	W	X
Y	Z		

a	b	c	d
e	f	g	h
i	j	k	l
m	n	o	p
q	r	s	t
u	v	w	x
y	z		

My name is ....

Underline the letters in your name.

A B C D E F G H I J K L M N O P Q R S T U V W X Y Z

a b c d e f g h i j k l m n o p q r s t u v w x y z

_____

His name is ....

Underline the letters in his name.

A B C D E F G H I J K L M N O P Q R S T U V W X Y Z

a b c d e f g h i j k l m n o p q r s t u v w x y z

_____

Her name is ....

Underline the letters in her name.

A B C D E F G H I J K L M N O P Q R S T U V W X Y Z

a b c d e f g h i j k l m n o p q r s t u v w x y z

My address is ....

....

....

....

Underline the letters in your address.

A B C D E F G H I J K L M N O P Q R S T U V W X Y Z

a b c d e f g h i j k l m n o p q r s t u v w x y z

Tam 's address is   2 South Drive

Longhill

Kent

KT 16 5 QZ

Underline the letters in Tam 's address.

A B C D E F G H I J K L M N O P Q R S T U V W X Y Z

a b c d e f g h i j k l m n o p q r s t u v w x y z

Numbers

•	1	one	_ _ _
• •	2	two	_ _ _
• • •	3	three	_ _ _ _ _
• • • •	4	four	_ _ _ _
• • • • • •	5	five	_ _ _ _
• • • • • •	6	six	_ _ _
• • • • • • •	7	seven	_ _ _ _ _
• • • • • • • •	8	eight	_ _ _ _ _
• • • • • • • •	9	nine	_ _ _ _ _
• • • • • • • •	10	ten	_ _ _

12

Numbers

11	eleven	ele_e_	_ _ _ _ _ _
12	twelve	tw_lv_	_ _ _ _ _ _
13	thirteen	th_ _t_ _n	_ _ _ _ _ _ _ _
14	fourteen	f_ur_ee_	_ _ _ _ _ _ _ _
15	fifteen	f_ft_ _n	_ _ _ _ _ _ _
16	sixteen	s_xt_ _ _	_ _ _ _ _ _
17	seventeen	s_v_n_een	_ _ _ _ _ _ _ _ _
18	eighteen	eig_ _ee_	_ _ _ _ _ _ _ _
19	nineteen	n_ne_ee_	_ _ _ _ _ _ _ _
20	twenty	t_ent_	_ _ _ _ _ _

13

1	one
2	two
3	three
4	four
5	five
6	six
7	seven
8	eight
9	nine
10	ten

11	eleven
12	twelve
13	thirteen
14	fourteen
15	fifteen
16	sixteen
17	seventeen
18	eighteen
19	nineteen
20	twenty

Numbers

2   one   5   three

nine   10   two   8

9   seven   4   six

five   3   ten   7

6   eight   1   four

1   one   _____

_____   _____

_____   _____

_____   _____

_____   _____

16

Numbers

11   sixteen   20   fourteen

twelve   18   seventeen   15

16   eleven   14   nineteen

twenty   17   eighteen   13

12   thirteen   19   fifteen

11   eleven   _____

_____   _____

_____   _____

_____   _____

_____   _____

Numbers

21	twenty-one	_____-___
22	twenty-two	_____-___
23	twenty-three	_____-_____
24	twenty-four	_____-____
25	twenty-five	_____-____
26	twenty-six	_____-___
27	twenty-seven	_____-_____
28	twenty-eight	_____-_____
29	twenty-nine	_____-____
30	thirty	_____
40	forty	_____
50	fifty	_____
60	sixty	_____
70	seventy	_____
80	eighty	_____
90	ninety	_____
100	one hundred	___ _____
101	one hundred and one	___ _____ ___ ___
1,000	one thousand	___ _____
1,000,000	one million	___ _____

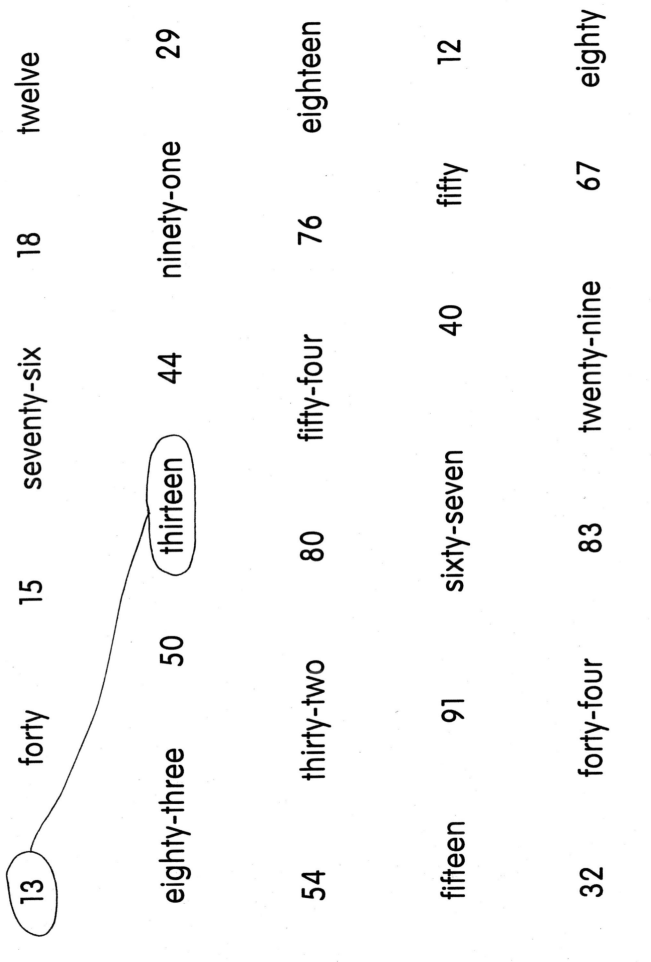

twelve

29

18

seventy-six

ninety-one

eighteen

44

fifty-four

76

fifty

15

thirteen

50

80

thirty-two

40

12

forty

sixty-seven

twenty-nine

67

eighty

eighty-three

91

83

54

fifteen

32

forty-four

13

(211)   nine hundred and thirty-one

390   one hundred and six

seven hundred and sixteen   448   (two hundred and eleven)   315

814   eight hundred and eighty-two   106   four hundred and forty-eight

six hundred   931   three hundred and ninety   123

565   three hundred and fifteen   716   eight hundred and fourteen

one hundred and twenty-three   882   five hundred and sixty-five   600

Numbers

1	one		1st	first
2	two		2nd	second
3	three		3rd	third
4	four		4th	fourth
5	five		5th	fifth
6	six		6th	sixth
7	seven		7th	seventh
8	eight		8th	eighth
9	nine		9th	ninth
10	ten		10th	tenth
11	eleven		11th	eleventh
12	twelve		12th	twelfth
13	thirteen		13th	thirteenth
14	fourteen		14th	fourteenth
15	fifteen		15th	fifteenth
16	sixteen		16th	sixteenth
17	seventeen		17th	seventeenth
18	eighteen		18th	eighteenth
19	nineteen		19th	nineteenth
20	twenty		20th	twentieth
21	twenty-one		21st	twenty-first
30	thirty		30th	thirtieth
40	forty		40th	fortieth
50	fifty		50th	fiftieth
60	sixty		60th	sixtieth
70	seventy		70th	seventieth
80	eighty		80th	eightieth
90	ninety		90th	ninetieth
100	one hundred		100th	one hundredth
101	one hundred and one		101st	one hundred and first
1,000	one thousand		1,000th	one thousandth
1,000,000	one million		1,000,000th	one millionth

How many ?

There is one mug.

There are two mugs.

There are three mugs.

There are four mugs.

There are five mugs.

How many ?

_____ __ _____ boy.

_____ __ _____ cakes.

_____ __ _____ keys.

_____ __ _____ birds.

_____ __ _____ umbrellas.

22

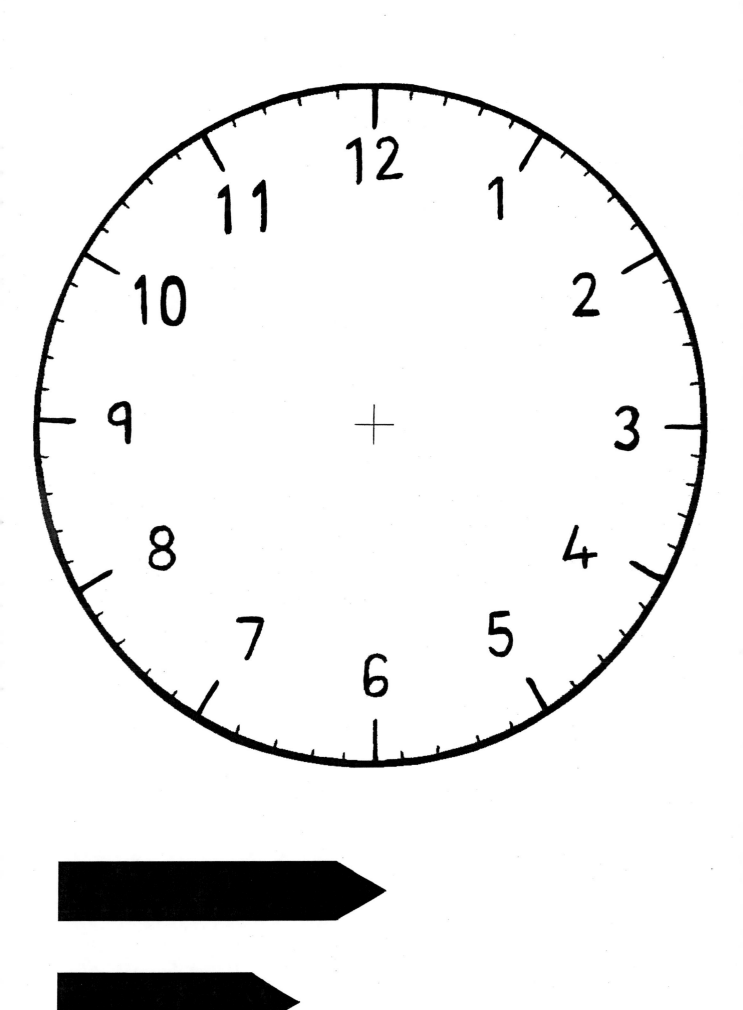

23

What time is it ?

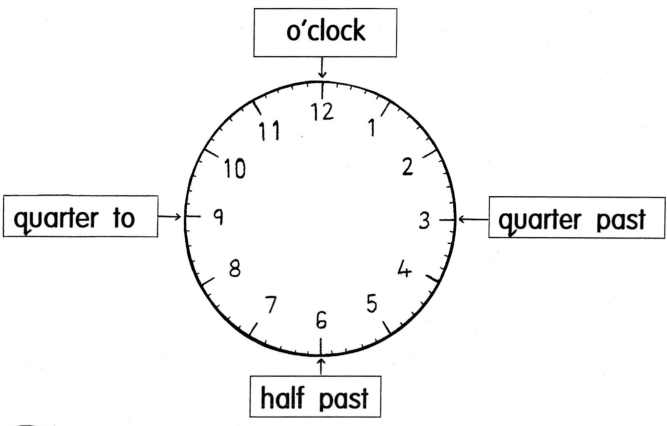

It is two o'clock.

It is quarter past seven.

It is half past ten.

It is quarter to four.

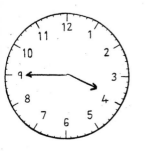

What time is it ?

It is _____

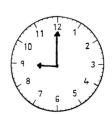

It is _____

It is _____

It is _____

It is _____

It is _____

It is _____

It is _____

25

What time is it ?

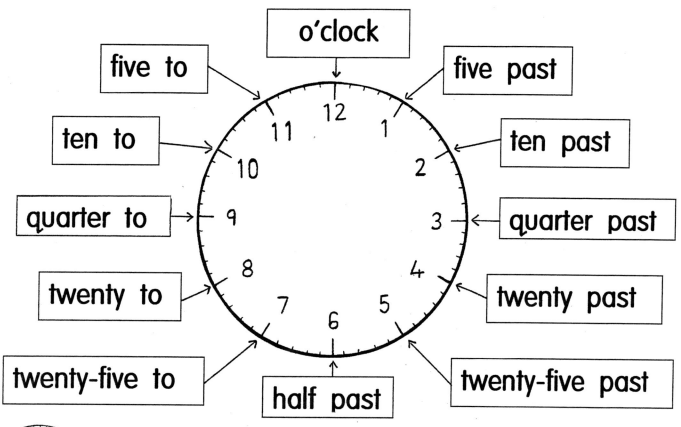

five to · o'clock · five past · ten to · ten past · quarter to · quarter past · twenty to · twenty past · twenty-five to · half past · twenty-five past

It is five past eight.

It is twenty past nine.

It is twenty-five to four.

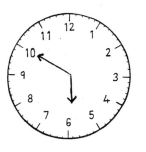

It is ten to six.

What time is it ?

 It is _____

 It is _____

 It is _____

 It is _____

 It is _____

 It is _____

 It is _____

 It is _____

27

What time is it ?

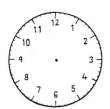 It is _____

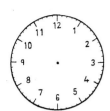 It is _____

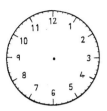 It is _____

 It is _____

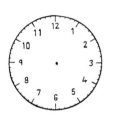 It is _____

 It is _____

 It is _____

 It is _____

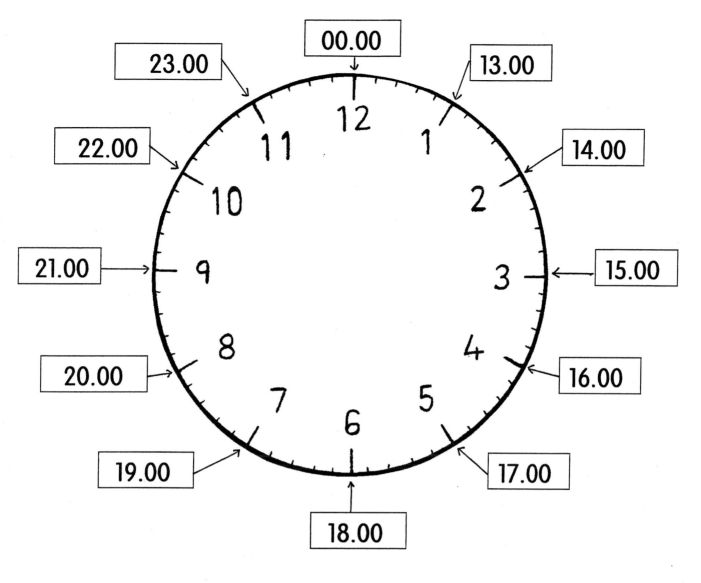

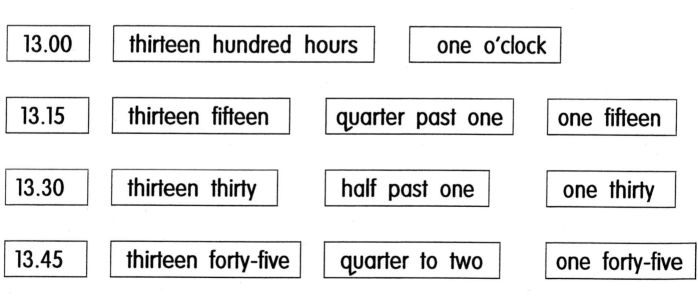

| a.m. | 00.01 - 12.00 | in the morning |
| p.m. | 12.01 - 24.00 | in the afternoon / in the evening / at night |

29

Days

Monday   M_n_ay   Mo_d_y   _ _ _ _ _ _

Tuesday   Tu_sd_y   T_e_ _a_   _ _ _ _ _ _ _

Wednesday   We_n_s_ay   W_d_e_d_ _   _ _ _ _ _ _ _ _ _

Thursday   T_u_s_a_   Th_r_d_y   _ _ _ _ _ _ _ _

Friday   Fr_d_y   F_i_a_   _ _ _ _ _ _

Saturday   S_t_r_a_   Sa_u_d_ _   _ _ _ _ _ _ _ _

Sunday   Su_d_y   S_n_ay   _ _ _ _ _ _

Today is   _ _ _ _ _ _ _ _ _ _ _ _

Yesterday was   _ _ _ _ _ _ _ _ _ _ _

Tomorrow will be   _ _ _ _ _ _ _ _ _ _

Days

Wednesday   Monday

Saturday   Thursday   Sunday

Friday   Tuesday

1. _____

2. _____

3. _____

4. _____

5. _____

6. _____

7. _____

Days

M _ _ d _ y

T _ _ s _ _ y

W _ _ n _ _ d a _

T _ _ r s _ _ y

F _ _ d _ _

S _ _ u _ d _ y

S _ _ d _ _

_ _ _ _ _ _

_ _ _ _ _ _ _

_ _ _ _ _ _ _ _ _

_ _ _ _ _ _ _ _

_ _ _ _ _ _

_ _ _ _ _ _ _ _

_ _ _ _ _ _

Months

January	J_n_a_y	Ja_u_r_	_ _ _ _ _ _ _
February	Fe_r_a_y	F_b_u_r_	_ _ _ _ _ _ _ _
March	M_r_h	Ma_c_	_ _ _ _ _
April	Ap_i_	A_r_l	_ _ _ _ _
May	M_y	Ma_	_ _ _
June	Ju_e	Ju_ _	_ _ _ _
July	J_l_	Ju_ _	_ _ _ _
August	Au_u_t	A_g_s_	_ _ _ _ _ _
September	S_p_e_b_r	Se_t_m_e_	_ _ _ _ _ _ _ _ _
October	Oc_o_e_	O_t_b_r	_ _ _ _ _ _ _
November	N_v_m_er	No_e_b_r	_ _ _ _ _ _ _ _
December	De_e_b_r	D_c_m_e_	_ _ _ _ _ _ _ _

Months

July   December   April

January   September   February

May   November   August

March   June   October

1. _____

2. _____

3. _____

4. _____

5. _____

6. _____

7. _____

8. _____

9. _____

10. _____

11. _____

12. _____

34

Months

J _ n _ _ ry

F _ b _ _ a r y

M _ r _ h

A _ r _ l

M _ y

J _ n _

J _ l _

A _ g _ st

S _ p t _ _ b _ r

O _ t _ b e _

N _ v _ m _ er

D e _ e _ b e _

_____

_ _ _ _ _ _

_ _ _ _ _ _ _ _

_ _ _ _ _

_ _ _ _ _

_ _ _

_ _ _ _

_ _ _ _

_ _ _ _ _

_ _ _ _ _ _ _ _ _

_ _ _ _ _ _ _

_ _ _ _ _ _ _

_ _ _ _ _ _ _ _

Monday	Tuesday
Wednesday	Thursday
Friday	Saturday
Sunday	

January	February
March	April
May	June
July	August
September	October
November	December

36

What is the date ?

	May		2000		
Monday	1	8	15	22	29
Tuesday	2	9	16	23	30
Wednesday	3	10	17	24	31
Thursday	4	11	18	25	
Friday	5	12	19	26	
Saturday	6	13	20	27	
Sunday	7	14	21	28	

It is Monday 1st May 2000.　　　　　　1 . 5 . 00

It is Sunday _ __ ___ ____.　　　　　7 . 5 . 00

It is _____ __ __ ___ ____.　　　10 . 5 . 00

It __ _____ __ __ ___ ____.　　　23 . 5 . 00

__ __ _____ __ __ ___ ____.　　　18 . 5 . 00

Today is _____ ___ _____ _____.

Yesterday was _____ ___ _____ _____.

Tomorrow will be _____ ___ _____ _____.

My birthday is _____ ___ _____ _____.

37

The seasons

spring   summer   autumn   winter

The weather

It's raining.	It's sunny.	It's cloudy.	It's snowing.
It's windy.	It's misty.	It's hot.	It's cold.

What is the weather like ?

_____

_____

_____

_____

_____

What is the weather like today ?

_____

What was the weather like yesterday ?

_____

Forms

Name _____

Address _____

_____

_____

_____

Telephone Number _____

_____

Surname _____

First Name _____

Address _____

_____

_____

_____

Telephone Number _____

_____

Surname _____

First Name _____

Address _____

_____

_____

Postcode _____

Telephone Number _____

4 C

CAPITAL LETTERS

NAME _____

ADDRESS _____

_____

_____

_____

TELEPHONE NUMBER _____

CAPITAL LETTERS

SURNAME _____

FIRST NAME _____

ADDRESS _____

_____

_____

_____

TELEPHONE NUMBER _____

CAPITAL LETTERS

SURNAME _____

FIRST NAME _____

ADDRESS _____

_____

_____

POSTCODE _____

TELEPHONE NUMBER _____

41

CAPITAL LETTERS

Surname _____ Mr / Mrs / Miss _____

First Name _____

Address _____

_____

_____

Postcode _____

Telephone Number _____

CAPITAL LETTERS

SURNAME _____ MR / MRS / MISS _____

FIRST NAME _____

ADDRESS _____

_____

_____

POSTCODE _____

TELEPHONE NUMBER _____

DATE OF BIRTH _____

CAPITAL LETTERS

SURNAME _____ MR / MRS / MISS _____

FIRST NAME _____

ADDRESS _____

_____

_____

POSTCODE _____

TELEPHONE NUMBER _____

DATE OF BIRTH _____

NATIONALITY _____

CAPITAL LETTERS

Surname _____   Mr / Mrs / Miss _____

First Name _____

Address _____

_____

_____

Postcode _____

Telephone Number _____

Date of Birth _____

Nationality _____

Occupation _____

Sex (please tick √)   Male   Female

Signature _____   Date _____

CAPITAL LETTERS

MR / MRS / MISS ☐☐☐   INITIALS ☐☐

SURNAME
ADDRESS

POSTCODE

43

Colours

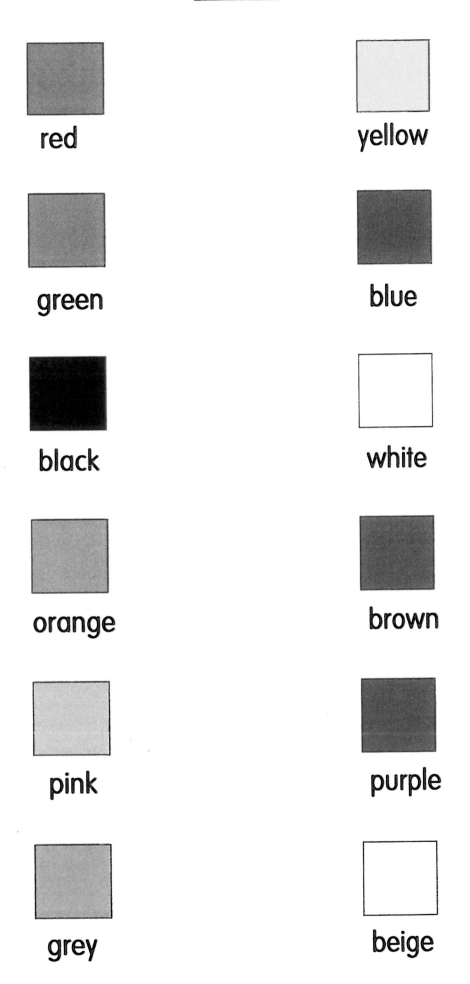

red	yellow
green	blue
black	white
orange	brown
pink	purple
grey	beige

44

Colours

red

yellow

green

blue

black

white

orange

brown

pink

purple

grey

beige

45

Colours

red   green   pink

yellow   black   purple

blue   grey   white

brown   orange   beige

_____   _____   _____

_____   _____   _____

_____   _____   _____

_____   _____   _____

46

Colours

red	green	pink
yellow	black	purple
blue	grey	white
brown	orange	beige

47

⬤ red	r _ d	_ ed	re _	_____
⚪ yellow	y_ll_w	ye_ _ow	_ello_	_____
⚪ green	g_een	gr_ _n	_ree_	_____
⬤ blue	b_ue	bl_e	_lu_	_____
⬤ black	b_a_k	bl_c_	_lac_	_____
⚪ white	wh_t_	w_i_e	_hit_	_____
⚪ orange	o_an_e	or_ng_	_ra_ _e	_____
⬤ brown	br_w_	b_o_n	_r_ _n	_____
⚪ pink	p_nk	pi_k	_ink	_____
⬤ purple	pu_pl_	p_r_le	_u_p_e	_____
⚪ grey	g_ey	gr_y	_re_	_____
⚪ beige	b_ig_	bei_e	_e_g_	_____

48

○	red	r _ d	_ ed	re _ _____
○	yellow	y_ll_w	ye_ _ow	_ello_ _____
○	green	g_een	gr_ _n	_ree_ _____
○	blue	b_ue	bl_e	_lu_ _____
○	black	b_a_k	bl_c_	_lac_ _____
○	white	wh_t_	w_i_e	_hit_ _____
○	orange	o_an_e	or_ng_	_ra_ _e _____
○	brown	br_w_	b_o_n	_r_ _n _____
○	pink	p_nk	pi_k	_ink _____
○	purple	pu_pl_	p_r_le	_u_p_e _____
○	grey	g_ey	gr_y	_re_ _____
○	beige	b_ig_	bei_e	_e_g_ _____

49

green	white	pink	beige
yellow	black	brown	grey
red	blue	orange	purple

green		yellow		red	
white		black		blue	
pink		brown		orange	
beige		grey		purple	

51

The face

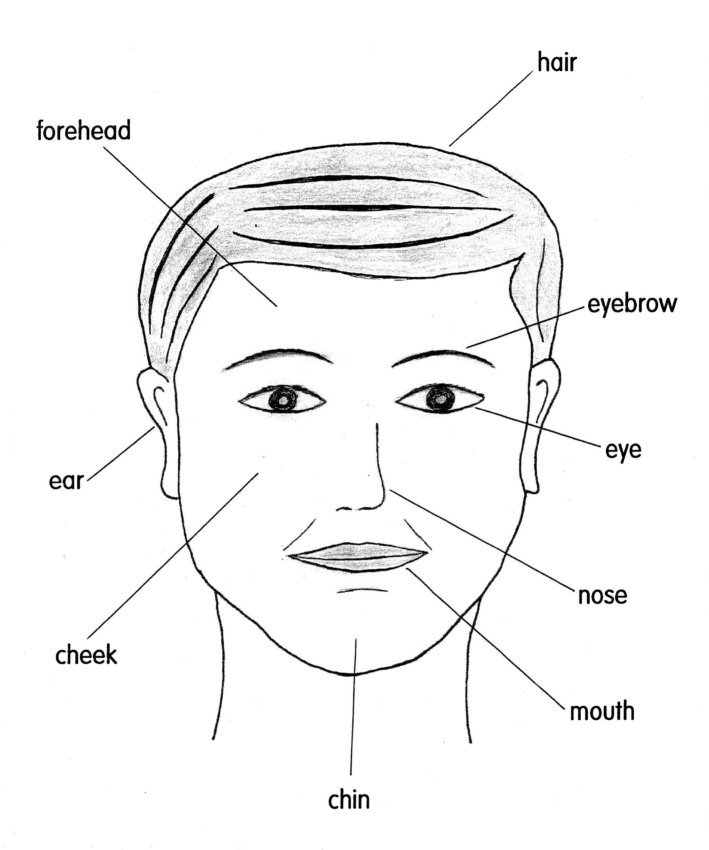

hair

forehead

eyebrow

eye

ear

nose

cheek

mouth

chin

The face

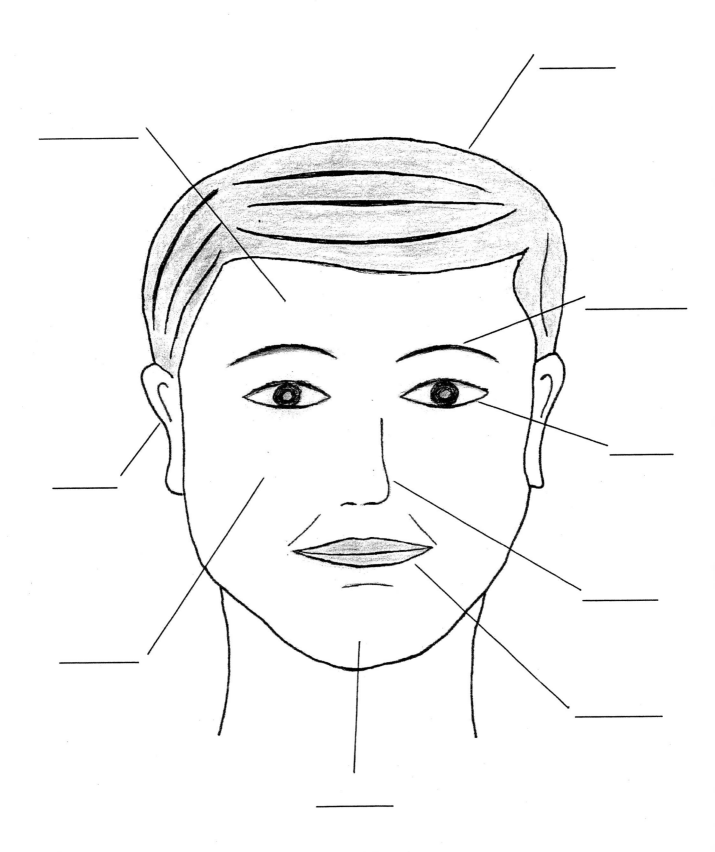

53

The body

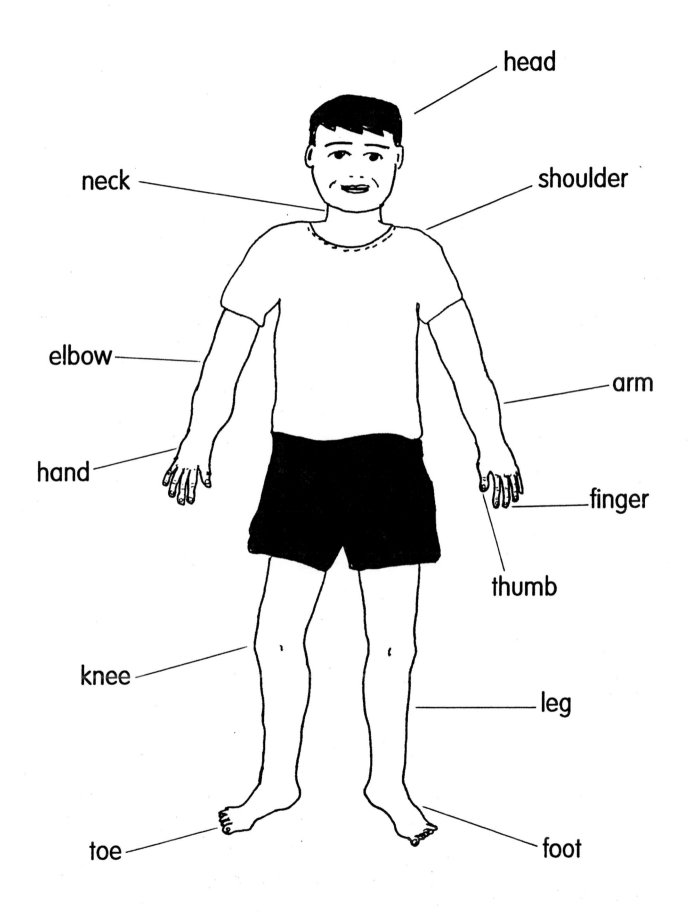

head

neck

shoulder

elbow

arm

hand

finger

thumb

knee

leg

toe

foot

5 4

The body

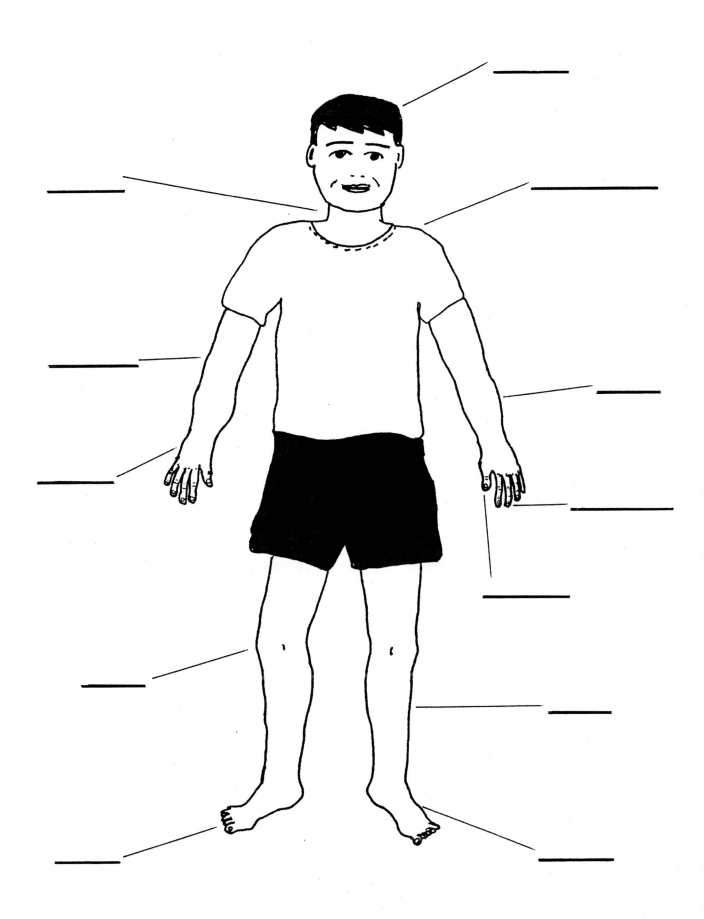

hand	leg	shoulder
knee	head	foot
finger	arm	neck
elbow	toe	thumb

nose	hair	cheek
ear	forehead	mouth
eye	chin	eyebrow

A family

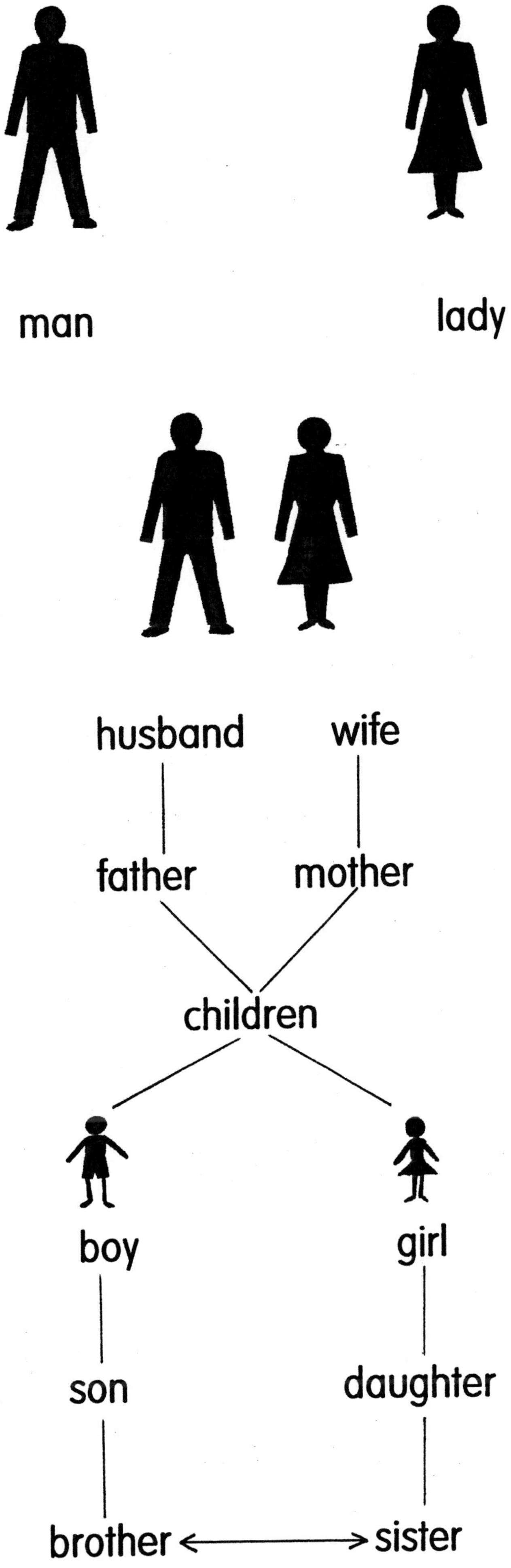

man   lady

husband   wife

father   mother

children

boy   girl

son   daughter

brother ←——————→ sister

A family

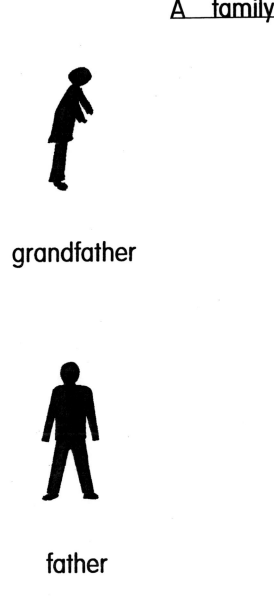

grandfather

grandmother

father

mother

grandson

granddaughter

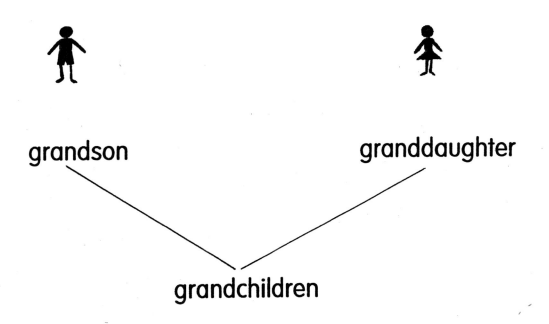

grandchildren

A family

_____   _____

_____   _____

_____   _____

_____

_____   _____

_____   _____

_____   _____

A family

_____

_____

_____

_____

_____

_____

_____

60

man	lady
husband	wife
father	mother
boy	girl
son	daughter
brother	sister
children	grandchildren
grandfather	grandmother
grandson	granddaughter

<u>My family</u>

My name is   _____

I have   _____ brother / brothers.

I have   _____ sister / sisters.

I have   _____ child / children.

I have   _____ son / sons.

I have   _____ daughter / daughters.

I have   _____ grandchild / grandchildren.

I have   _____ grandson / grandsons.

I have   _____ granddaughter / granddaughters.

Clothes

trousers	jeans	jumper
shirt	blouse	skirt
dress	jacket	socks

63

Clothes

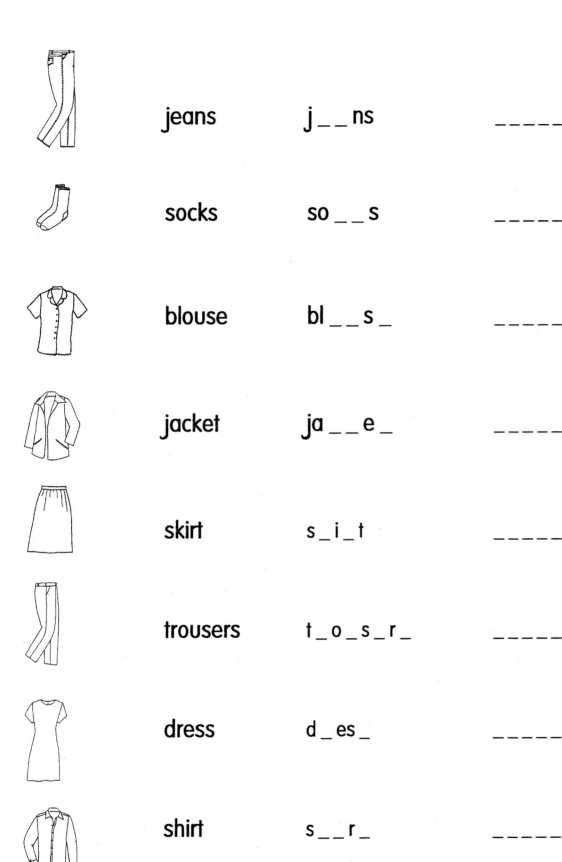

jeans   j _ _ ns   _ _ _ _ _

socks   so _ _ s   _ _ _ _ _

blouse   bl _ _ s _   _ _ _ _ _ _

jacket   ja _ _ e _   _ _ _ _ _ _

skirt   s _ i _ t   _ _ _ _ _

trousers   t _ o _ s _ r _   _ _ _ _ _ _ _ _

dress   d _ es _   _ _ _ _ _

shirt   s _ _ r _   _ _ _ _ _

jumper   j _ m _ e _   _ _ _ _ _ _

64

Clothes

socks   blouse   jacket

jumper   skirt   jeans

trousers   shirt   dress

_____

_____

_____

_____

_____

_____

_____

_____

_____

What are they wearing ?

The lady is wearing a _ _ _ _ _ .

She is wearing _____ .

The man is wearing a _ _ _ _ _ _ and a _ _ _ _ _ and _ _ _ _ _ _ _ _ .

He is wearing _____ .

The girl is wearing a _ _ _ _ _ _ and a _ _ _ _ _ and _ _ _ _ _ .

She _____ .

The boy is wearing a _ _ _ _ _ _ and _ _ _ _ _ .

He _____ .

66

Clothes

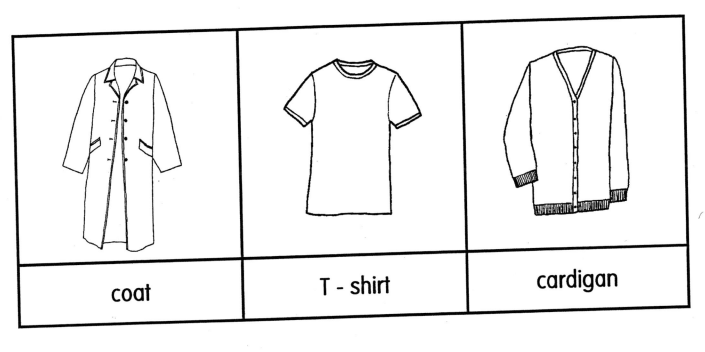

| coat | T - shirt | cardigan |

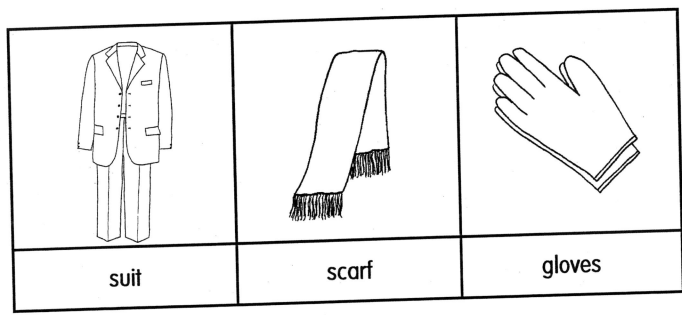

| suit | scarf | gloves |

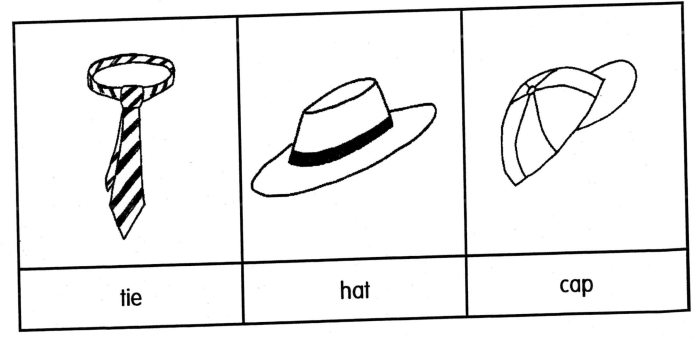

| tie | hat | cap |

67

Clothes

 hat   h _ t   _ _ _

 suit   s _ it   _ _ _ _

 T - shirt   T – s _ i _ t   _ _ _ _ _ _ _

 gloves   g _ ov _ s   _ _ _ _ _ _

 coat   co _ t   _ _ _ _

 tie   ti _   _ _ _

 cap   c _ p   _ _ _

 cardigan   ca _ d _ g _ n   _ _ _ _ _ _ _ _

 scarf   s _ a _ f   _ _ _ _ _

Clothes

suit	cap	gloves
tie	coat	hat
scarf	cardigan	T - shirt

_____

_____

_____

_____

_____

_____

_____

_____

_____

69

What are they wearing ?

The lady is wearing a ____ and a _____ and a ___ and _____.

She is wearing _____.

The man is wearing a ____ and a _____ and a ___.

He is wearing _____.

The girl is wearing a _____ and a _____.

She _____.

The boy is wearing a _-_____ and _____ and a ___.

He _____.

70

Clothes

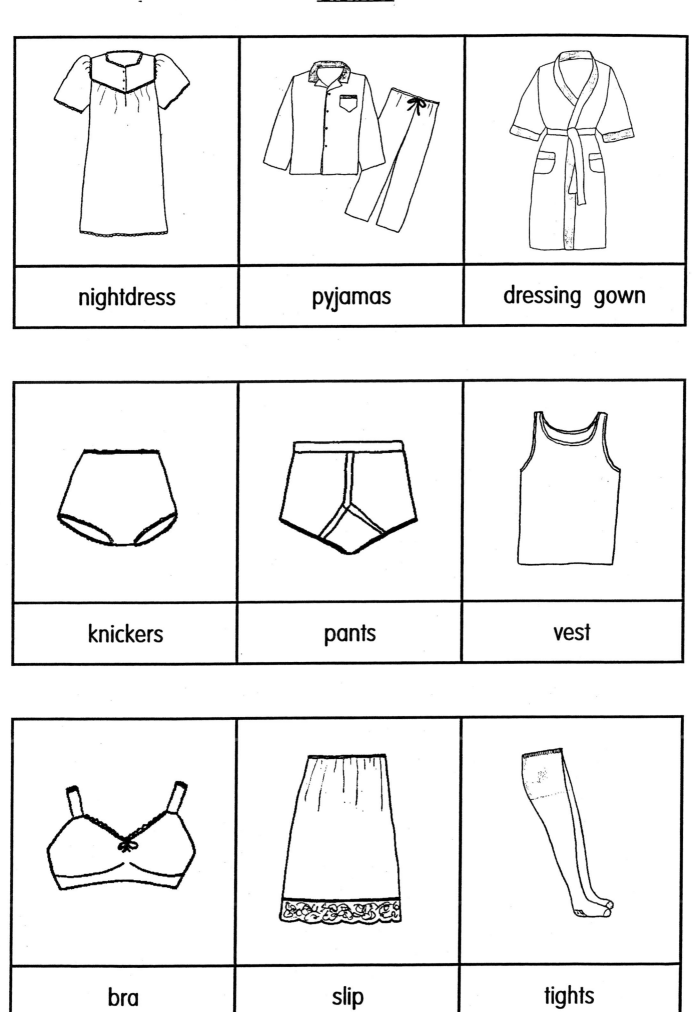

nightdress	pyjamas	dressing gown
knickers	pants	vest
bra	slip	tights

Clothes

 vest   ve _ t   _ _ _ _

 slip   s _ ip   _ _ _ _

 pyjamas   p _ j _ m _ s   _ _ _ _ _ _ _

 bra   b _ a   _ _ _

 nightdress   ni _ htd _ es _   _ _ _ _ _ _ _ _ _ _

 pants   pa _ t _   _ _ _ _ _

 tights   t _ g _ ts   _ _ _ _ _ _

 dressing gown

      d _ e _ si _ g go _ n   _ _ _ _ _ _ _ _ _ _ _ _ _

 knickers   k _ i _ ker _   _ _ _ _ _ _ _ _

72

Clothes

tights	vest	bra
pants	pyjamas	slip
dressing gown	nightdress	knickers

_____   _____   _____

_____   _____   _____

_____   _____   _____

What are they wearing ?

The lady is wearing a ___ and _____ and a ____.

She is wearing _____.

The man is wearing _____ and a _____ ____.

He is wearing _____.

The girl is wearing a _____ and _____.

She _____.

The boy is wearing a ____ and _____.

He _____.

The baby is wearing a _____.

She _____.

74

What are you wearing ?

Are you wearing   _ _ _ _ _ ?   _ _ _ _ _

Are you wearing a   _ _ _ _ _ _ ?   _ _ _ _ _

Are you wearing a   _ _ _ _ _ _ ?   _ _ _ _ _

Are you wearing   _ _ _ _ _ ?   _ _ _ _ _

Are you wearing a   _ _ _ _ _ ?   _ _ _ _ _

Are you wearing a   _ _ _ _ _ _ ?   _ _ _ _ _

Are you wearing   _ _ _ _ _ _ _ _ ?   _ _ _ _ _

Are you wearing a   _ _ _ _ ?   _ _ _ _ _

Are you wearing a   _ _ _ _ _ ?   _ _ _ _ _

Are you wearing   _ _ _ _ _ _ ?   _ _ _ _ _

75

Shoes

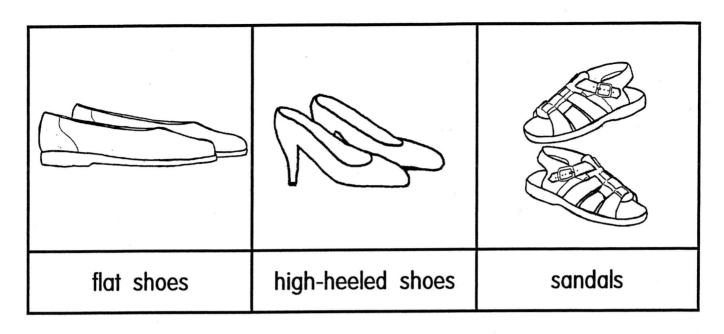

flat shoes	high-heeled shoes	sandals

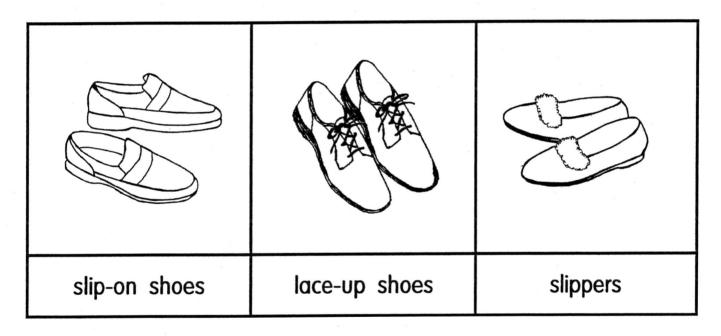

slip-on shoes	lace-up shoes	slippers

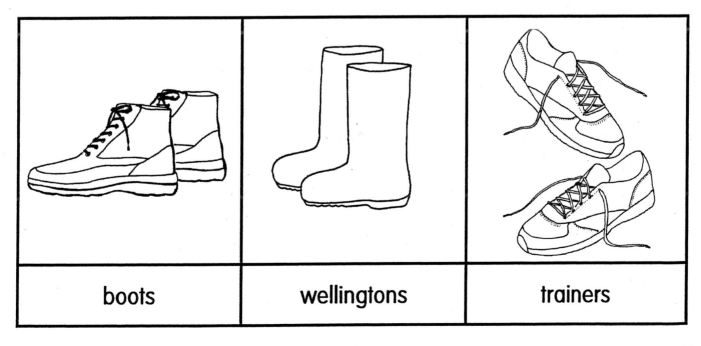

boots	wellingtons	trainers

Shoes

 trainers   t_a_ n_r_   _ _ _ _ _ _ _ _

 high-heeled shoes   hi_h-he_l_d sh_es   _ _ _ _-_ _ _ _ _ _ _ _ _ _ _

 boots   b _ _ t _   _ _ _ _ _

 lace-up shoes   l _ c _ - up s _ o _ s   _ _ _ _-_ _ _ _ _ _ _

 wellingtons   we _ l _ n _ t _ ns   _ _ _ _ _ _ _ _ _ _

 slip-on shoes   s _ _ p - o _ sh _ e _   _ _ _ _-_ _ _ _ _ _ _

 sandals   sa _ d _ l _   _ _ _ _ _ _ _

 flat shoes   f _ a _   s _ _ es   _ _ _ _ _ _ _ _ _

 slippers   s _ ip _ e _ s   _ _ _ _ _ _ _ _

Shoes

sandals	boots	lace-up shoes
high-heeled shoes	trainers	slip-on shoes
wellingtons	slippers	flat shoes

_____   _____   _____

_____   _____   _____

_____   _____   _____

House and garden

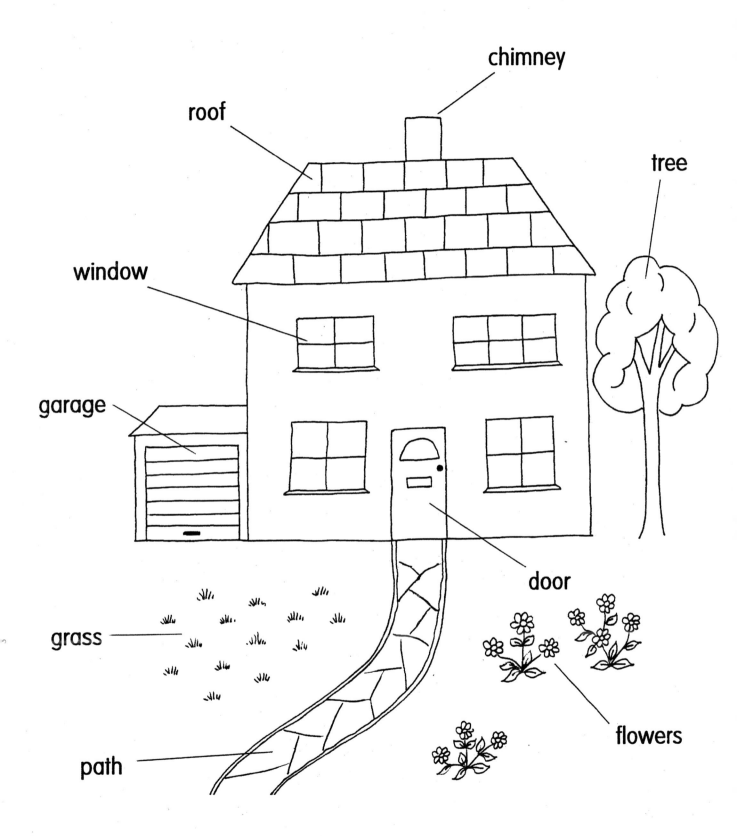

chimney

roof

tree

window

garage

grass

path

door

flowers

79

House and garden

window	chimney	flowers
grass	tree	roof
garage	door	path

The living room

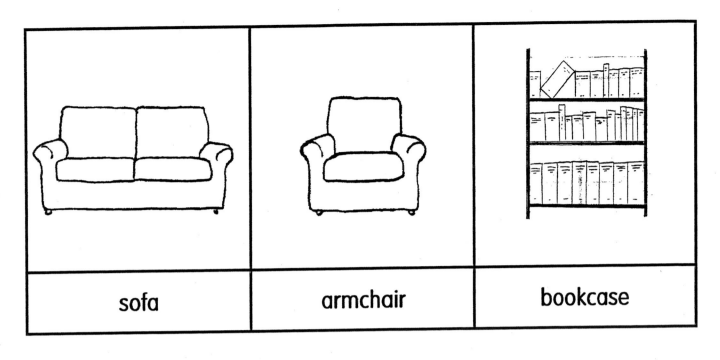

| sofa | armchair | bookcase |

| table | chair | carpet |

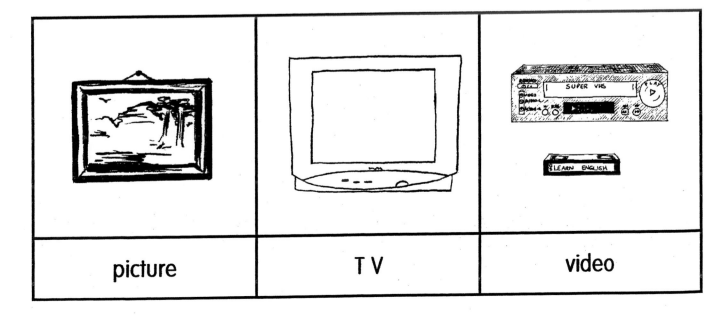

| picture | T V | video |

The bedroom

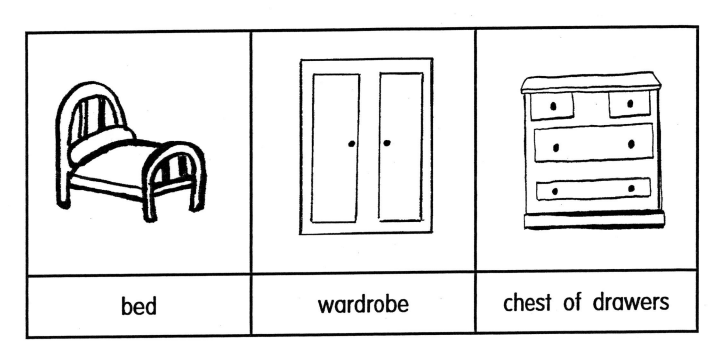

| bed | wardrobe | chest of drawers |

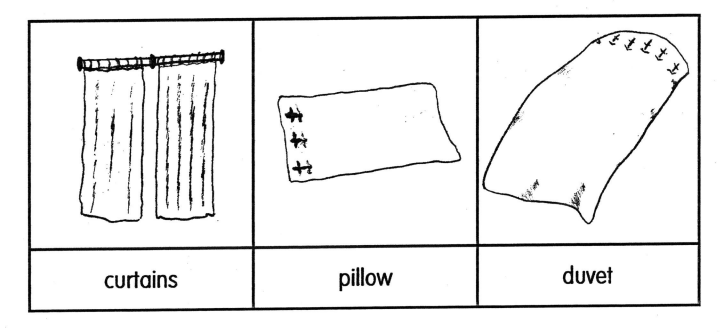

| curtains | pillow | duvet |

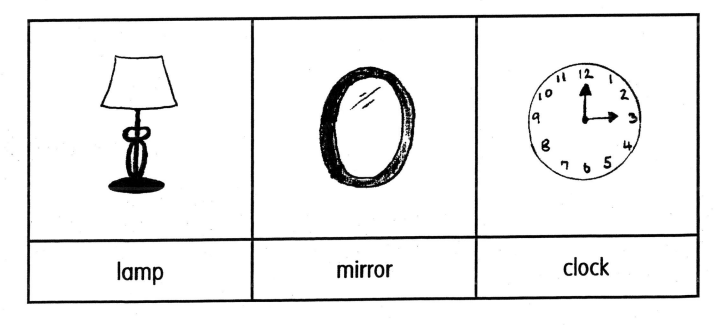

| lamp | mirror | clock |

What is in your living room ?

In my living room there is a _____.

In my living room there is a _____.

In my living room there is a _____.

What is in your bedroom ?

In my bedroom there is a _____.

In my bedroom there is a _____.

In my bedroom there is a _____.

The   kitchen

| cooker | sink | fridge |

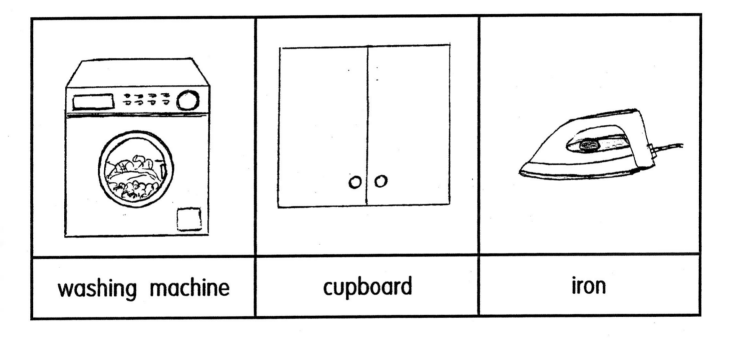

| washing machine | cupboard | iron |

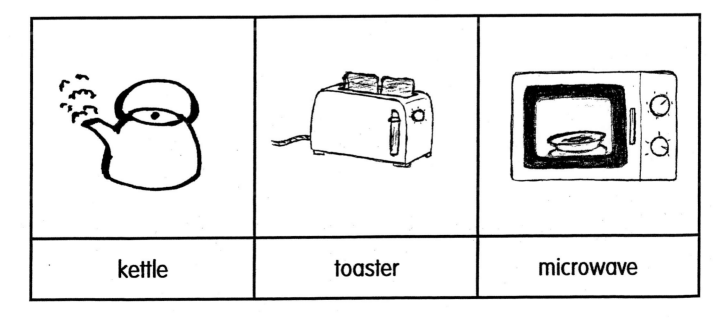

| kettle | toaster | microwave |

84

The bathroom

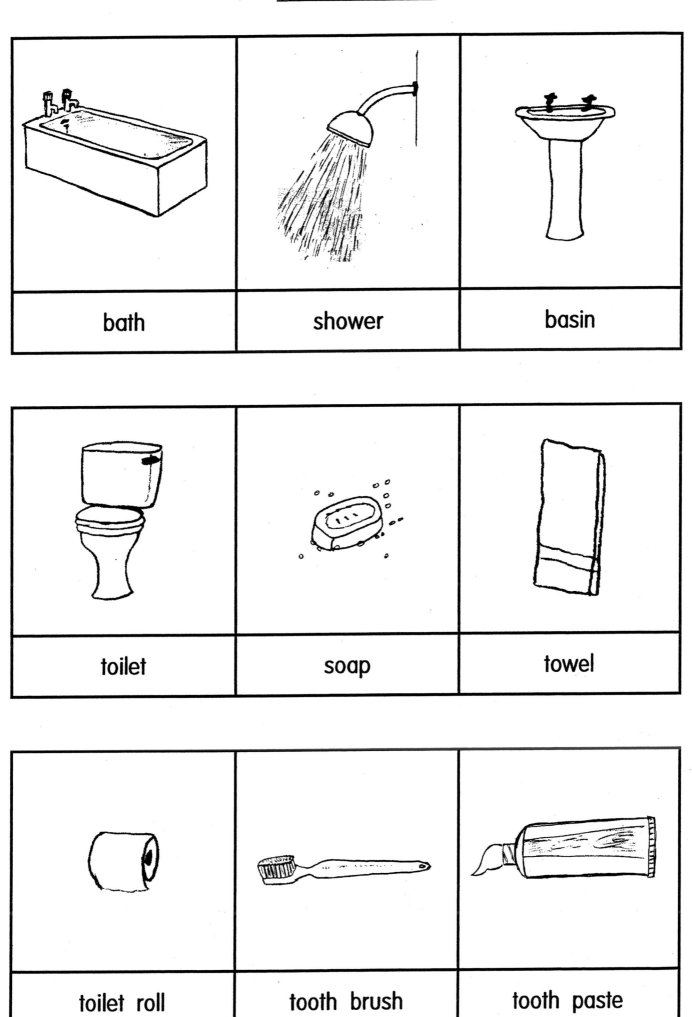

bath	shower	basin
toilet	soap	towel
toilet roll	tooth brush	tooth paste

85

What is in your kitchen ?

In my kitchen there is a _____.

In my kitchen there is a _____.

In my kitchen there is a _____.

What is in your bathroom ?

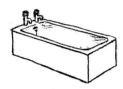

In my bathroom there is a _____.

In my bathroom there is a _____.

In my bathroom there is a _____.

86

In the kitchen

cup	saucer	plate
mug	bowl	glass
knife	fork	spoon

Rooms

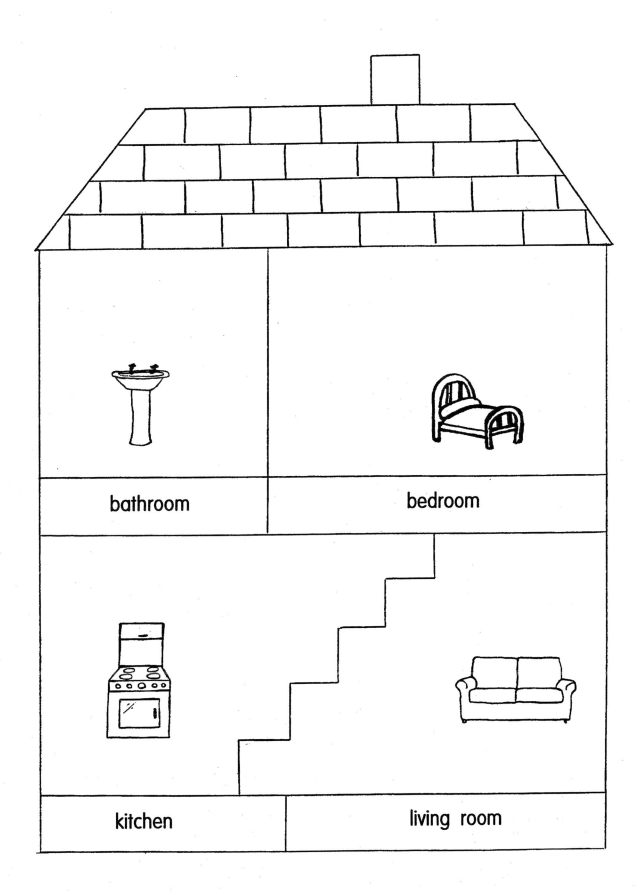

stairs	chair
cooker	bed
washing machine	wardrobe
sink	chest of drawers
fridge	basin
sofa	shower
armchair	toilet
table	bath

89

Food

bread	meat	chicken
fish	eggs	cheese
rice	chips	sandwiches

Food

bread   b _ e _ d   br _ a _   _ _ _ _ _

meat   me _ t   m _ a _   _ _ _ _

chicken   c _ i _ k _ n   ch _ c _ en   _ _ _ _ _ _ _

fish   fi _ h   f _ s _   _ _ _ _

eggs   e _ g _   eg _ s   _ _ _ _

cheese   ch _ e _ e   c _ e _ s _   _ _ _ _ _ _

rice   r _ c _   ri _ e   _ _ _ _

chips   ch _ p _   c _ i _ s   _ _ _ _ _

sandwiches s _ ndw _ c _ es sa _ d _ ich _ s _ _ _ _ _ _ _ _ _ _

Food and Drink

| tea | coffee | milk |

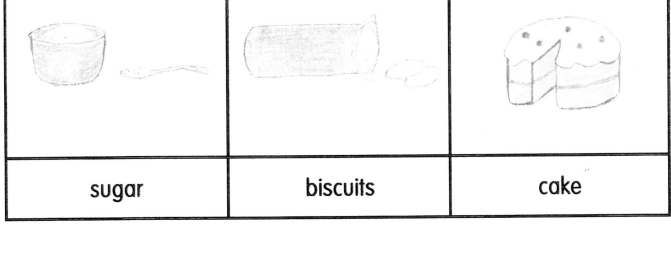

| sugar | biscuits | cake |

| chocolate | orange juice | cornflakes |

92

Food and Drink

tea   t _ a   te _   _ _ _

coffee   co _ f _ e   c _ f _ e _   _ _ _ _ _ _

milk   m _ l _   mi _ k   _ _ _ _

sugar   su _ a _   s _ g _ r   _ _ _ _ _ _

biscuits   b _ s _ u _ ts   bi _ c _ i _ s   _ _ _ _ _ _ _ _

cake   ca _ e   c _ k _   _ _ _ _

chocolate   c _ o _ ola _ e   ch _ c _ l _ t _ _ _ _ _ _ _ _ _ _

orange juice or _ nge ju _ ce o _ a _ ge j _ ice _ _ _ _ _ _ _ _ _ _ _

cornflakes   c _ rnf _ a _ e _ co _ n _ l _ k _ s _ _ _ _ _ _ _ _ _

What do you eat ?

I eat _____.

I eat _____.

I eat _____.

I don't eat _____.

I don't eat _____.

I don't eat _____.

What do you drink ?

I drink _____.

I drink _____.

I drink _____.

I don't drink _____.

I don't drink _____.

I don't drink _____.

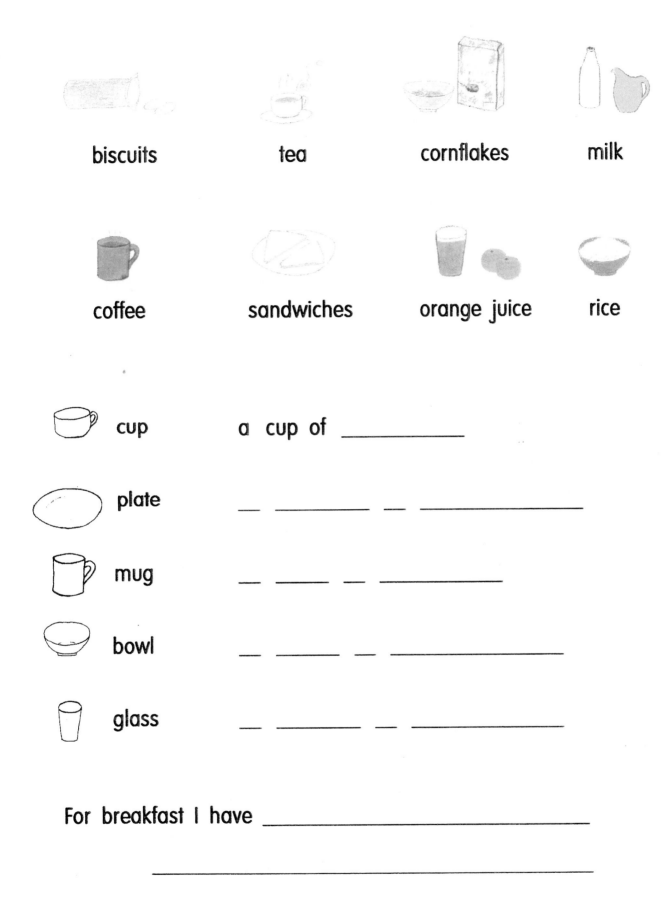

biscuits

tea

cornflakes

milk

coffee

sandwiches

orange juice

rice

cup   a cup of _____

plate   __ _____ __ _____

mug   __ ____ __ _____

bowl   __ _____ __ _____

glass   __ _____ __ _____

For breakfast I have _____

_____

Fruit

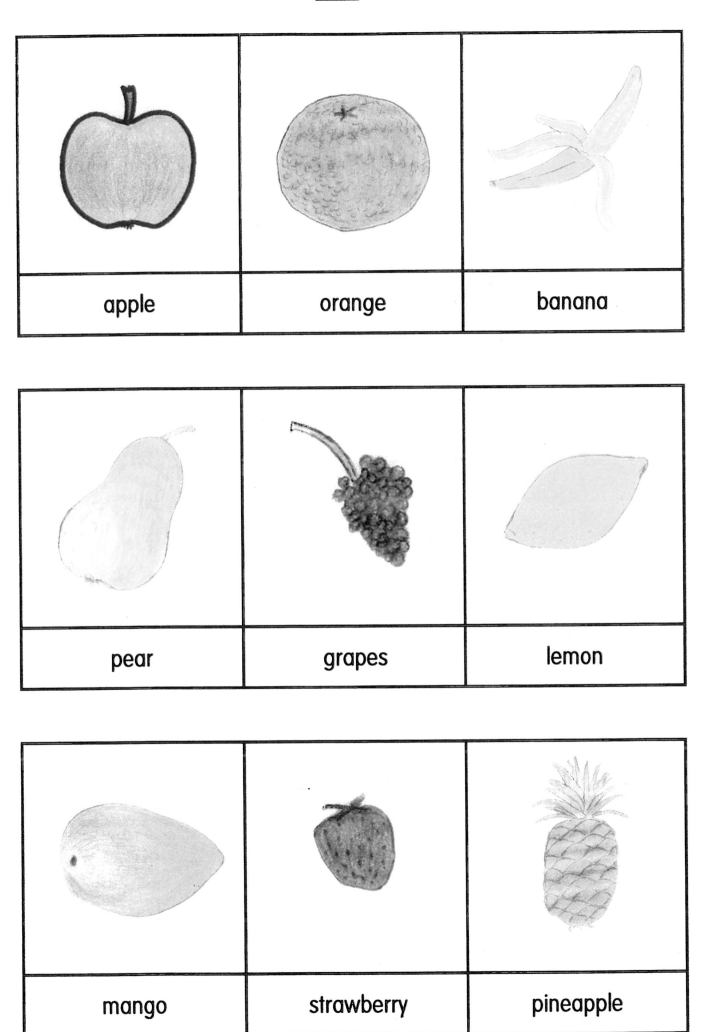

apple	orange	banana
pear	grapes	lemon
mango	strawberry	pineapple

96

Fruit

apple	ap _ l _	a _ p _ e	_ _ _ _ _
orange	o _ a _ g _	or _ n _ e	_ _ _ _ _ _
banana	ba _ a _ a	b _ n _ n _	_ _ _ _ _ _
pear	p _ a _	pe _ r	_ _ _ _
grapes	gr _ p _ s	g _ a _ es	_ _ _ _ _ _
lemon	l _ m _ n	le _ o _	_ _ _ _ _
mango	m _ n _ o	ma _ g _	_ _ _ _ _
strawberry	st _ awb _ rry	s _ r _ w _ e _ r _	_ _ _ _ _ _ _ _ _ _
pineapple	pin _ app _ e	pi _ e _ p _ le	_ _ _ _ _ _ _ _ _

97

What do you like ?

 apples

 oranges

 bananas

 pears

 grapes

 lemons

 mangos

 strawberries

 pineapples

I like _____.

I like _____.

I like _____.

I don't like _____.

I don't like _____.

I don't like _____.

98

Vegetables

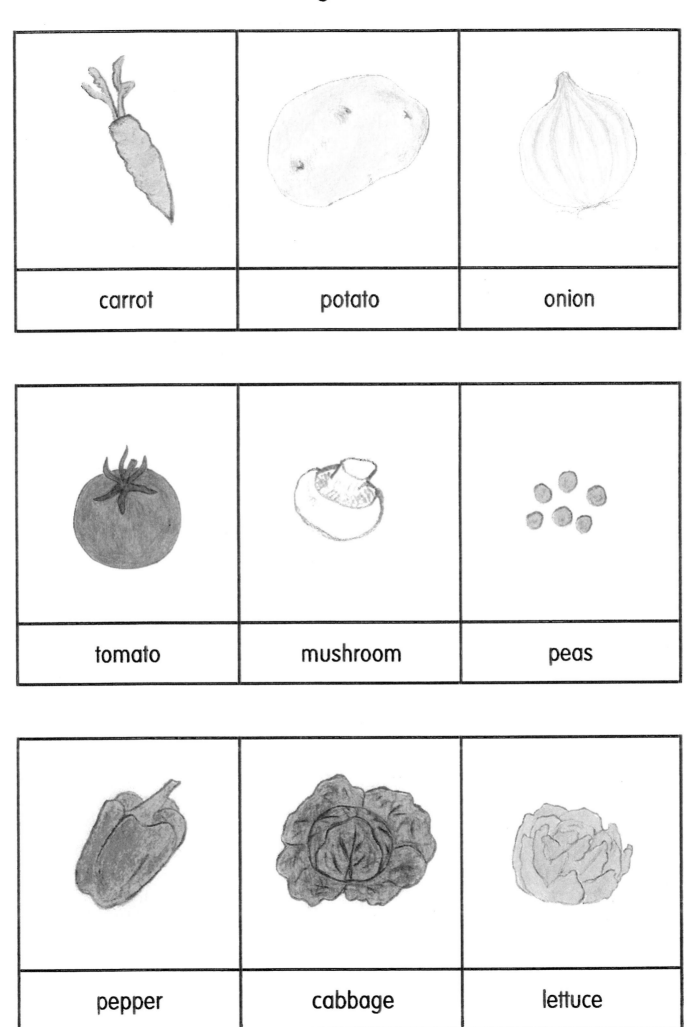

carrot	potato	onion
tomato	mushroom	peas
pepper	cabbage	lettuce

<u>Vegetables</u>

carrot   ca _ r _ t   c _ r _ o _   _ _ _ _ _ _

potato   p _ t _ t _   po _ a _ o   _ _ _ _ _ _

onion   on _ o _   o _ i _ _   _ _ _ _ _

tomato   t _ m _ t _   to _ a _ o   _ _ _ _ _ _

mushroom   m _ shr _ o _   mu _ h _ o _ m   _ _ _ _ _ _ _ _

peas   pe _ s   p _ a _   _ _ _ _

pepper   pe _ p _ r   p _ p _ e _   _ _ _ _ _ _

cabbage   ca _ b _ g _   c _ b _ a _ e   _ _ _ _ _ _ _

lettuce   l _ t _ u _ e   le _ t _ c _   _ _ _ _ _ _ _

What do you like ?

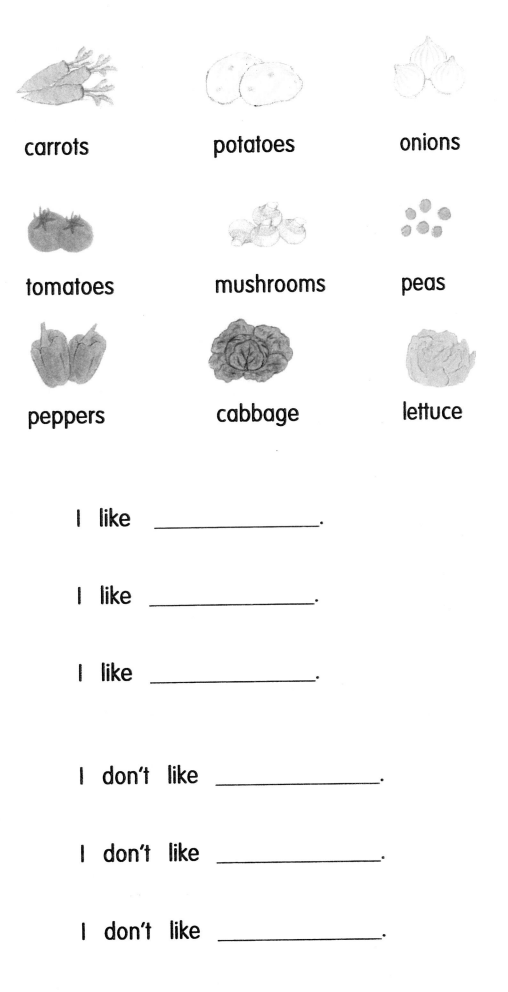

carrots potatoes onions

tomatoes mushrooms peas

peppers cabbage lettuce

I like _____.

I like _____.

I like _____.

I don't like _____.

I don't like _____.

I don't like _____.

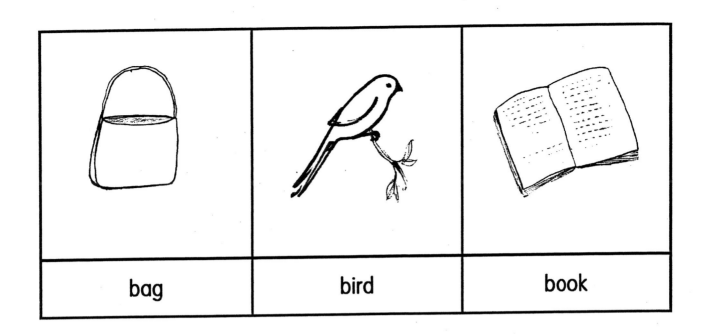

bag	bird	book

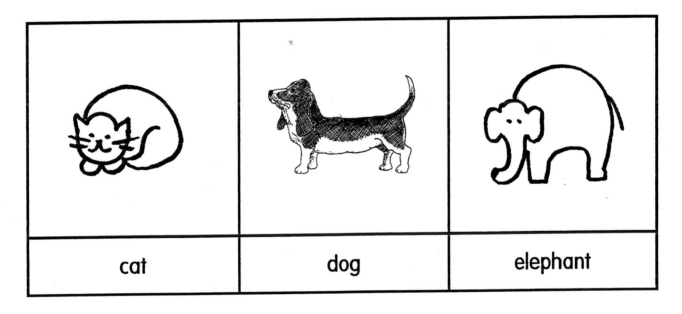

cat	dog	elephant

envelope	gate	glasses

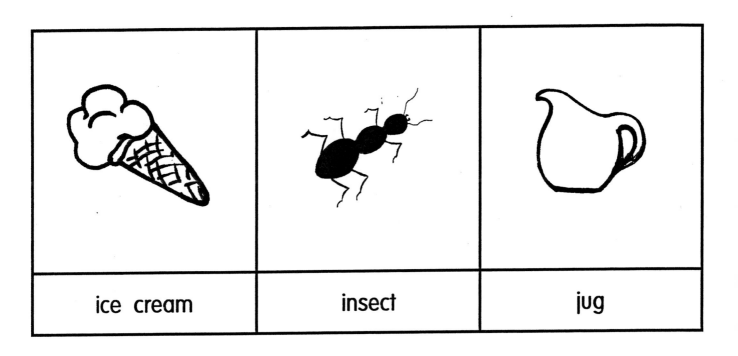

ice cream	insect	jug

key	lorry	money

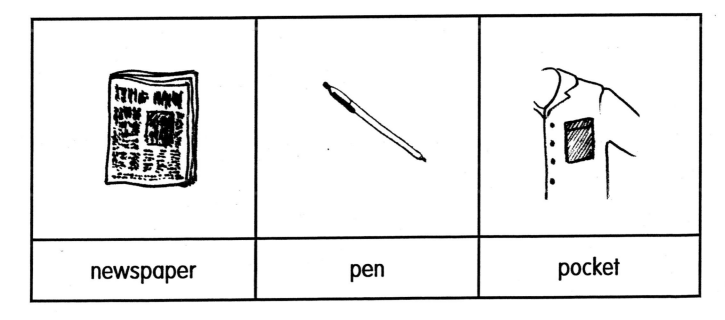

newspaper	pen	pocket

purse	queen	radio
ring	sun	tap
umbrella	watch	zip

104

Possessions

ring	umbrella	radio
glasses	purse	watch
book	money	key
envelope	pen	bag

_____   _____   _____

_____   _____   _____

_____   _____   _____

_____   _____   _____

a	e	i	o	u

 What's this ?   It's a banana.

 What's this ?   It's an apple.

 What's this ?   It's _____ cat.

 What's this ?   It's _____ umbrella.

 What's this ?   It's _____ jug.

 What's this ?   It's _____ elephant.

 What's this ?   It's _____ armchair.

 What's this ?   It's _____ pocket.

 What's this ?   It's _____ orange.

 What's this ?   It's _____ zip.

 What's this ?   It's _____ lorry.

 What's this ?   It's _____ ice cream.

106

S s	J j	H h	P p
B b	W w	U u	Q q
M m	K k	L l	T t

Vv	Ee	Aa	Pp
Bb	Ss	Dd	Hh
Ii	Cc	Tt	Ff

108

I i

Z z

C c

R r

2 South Drive
Longhill
Kent
KT 16 5 QZ

G g

A a

B b

E e

D d

F f

O o

M m

September
M T W T F S S

M T W T F S S

November
M T W T F S S

P p	1st January .... 31st December
K k	
J j	
L l	9
N n	
G g	
N n	
Y y	
C c	
T t	
W w	
R r	

Domino word list

A	address	L	lady
A	apple	L	lorry
B	bed	M	man
B	bird	M	mug
B	boy	N	newspaper
C	cake	N	nine
C	cat	O	October
C	coat	P	picture
D	dog	P	pocket
D	door	P	purse
E	elephant	Q	queen
E	envelope	R	radio
F	finger	R	ring
F	fork	S	soap
G	gate	S	sun
G	girl	T	table
H	hand	T	tap
H	house	T	toes
I	ice cream	U	umbrella
I	insect	V	video
J	jacket	W	watch
J	jug	W	window
K	kettle	Y	year
K	key	Z	zip